H-13 Si

By Wayne Mutza

Color By Don Greer

Illustrated By Randle Toepfer

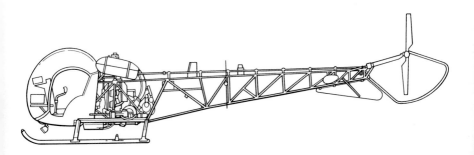

Mini Number 6

squadron/signal publications

A Bell H-13E makes a approach for landing at an Mobile Army Surgical Hospital (MASH) unit in Korea. The H-13 could carry two wounded soldiers.

Acknowledgements

Regina Burns, US Army Aviation Museum
Melvin Edwards
Ray Burdette
Keith and Donna Lovern
Lennart Lundh
Terry Love
Bob Steinbrunn
Nick Williams
Ron Williamson
Ned Gilliand
William Skerrett, NASA
Norm Taylor
Bell Helicopter Textron, Inc.
US Coast Guard
US Navy
MAP

A H-13E lands at a Mobile Army Surgical Hospital (MASH) unit to deliver a wounded soldier. Just as the Bell UH-1 Huey became the symbol of the Vietnam war, the Bell H-13 was the visible symbol of the Korean Conflict.

ISBN 0-89747-329-0

If you have any photographs of aircraft, armor, soldiers or ships of any nation, particularly wartime snapshots, why not share them with us and help make Squadron/Signal's books all the more interesting and complete in the future. Any photograph sent to us will be copied and the original returned. The donor will be fully credited for any photos used. Please send them to

Если у вас есть фотографии самолётов, вооружения, солдат или кораблей любой страны, особенно, снимки времён войны, поделитесь с нами и помогите сделать новые книги издательства Эскадрон/Сигнал ещё интереснее. Мы переснимем ваши фотографии и вернём оригиналы. Имена приславших снимки будут сопровождать все опубликованные фотографии. Присылайте, пожалуйста, фотографии по адресу:

軍用機、装甲車両、兵士、軍艦などの写真を所持しておられる方はいらっしゃいませんか？どの国のものでも結構です。作戦中に撮影されたものが特に良いのです。Squadron/Signal社の出版する刊行物において、このような写真は内容を一層充実し、興味深くすることができます。当方にお送り頂いた写真は、複写の後お返しいたします。出版物中に写真を使用した場合は、必ず提供者のお名前を明記させて頂きます。お写真は下記にご送付ください。

Squadron/Signal Publications, Inc.
1115 Crowley Drive
Carrollton, TX 75011-5010 USA

Introduction

The events that led to the monumental achievements of the Bell Model 47 began during 1930, when an inventor named Arthur Young began private helicopter research. During the fifteen years he devoted to creating the Bell Model 47, Young experimented with a variety of scale flying models. After learning from Igor Sikorsky that a tail rotor would counter torque, Young concentrated on improving stability. After numerous experiments, he invented a stabilizer bar which was linked directly to the rotor to function as a flywheel. This kept the action of the rotor blades independent from fuselage movement. The stabilizer bar solved the stability problem and became a traditional fixture on thousands of future Bell helicopters.

Aircraft companies showed little interest in Young's ideas until a demonstration at the Bell Aircraft Company on 3 September 1941. At that time, Bell, which had been founded in Buffalo, New York by Lawrence Bell in 1935, had been actively producing P-39 Airacobra fighters. Larry Bell liked Young's concept and the two agreed to construct two prototypes, beginning in late November of 1941. Labeled Experimental Model 30s, they were proof-of-concept predecessors to the Model 47. A small group of engineers broke away from the main plant in June 1942 and converted an old garage in Gardenville, New York into Bell's first helicopter plant.

Christened *Genevieve*, the first Model 30 was rolled out in December of 1942. After months of tethered flight and vibration problems, the Model 30 made its first free flight on 26 June 1943. The second prototype was completed that same year, followed by a third, which made its first flight on 25 April 1945.

The first Model 30 was initially built as a single-seat aircraft with four legs of aluminum tubing. By early 1943, wheels had replaced the legs and the fuselage and tail boom were covered. Ship No. 2, a fully covered two-seat aircraft with an enclosed cabin, had the distinction of being the first helicopter used by a doctor on a mercy mission. It was also the first Bell helicopter to make a rescue when a Bell pilot flew onto Lake Erie in March of 1945 to pick up two fishermen stranded on an ice floe.

The first two Model 30s were purposely built to resemble airplanes or automobiles, while the third ship was designed as a practical concept. Improvements in Ship No. 3 included a four-wheel landing gear, an advanced instrument panel, and a tubular tail boom. For a cockpit enclosure, Young invented a protective 'bubble', formed from Plexiglas, which became the classic trademark of the Model 47.

During the final months of the Second World War, when fighter aircraft production diminished, Larry Bell turned his attention to the helicopter as the company's future. In June of 1945, Bell began work on the first

Bell Aircraft Model 30 No. 1, named *Genevieve*, is rolled out of Bell's garage in December of 1942. The Model 30 was equipped with wheeled landing gear and a Blue fuselage covering. (Bell)

The second Model 30 was used to demonstrate the helicopter's potential. This demonstration flight was for the Civil Air Patrol at the Buffalo, New York Armory on 10 May 1944. (Bell)

Model 47, which was rolled out and flown six months later, on 8 December. It was followed by ten aircraft built for testing, training, and demonstration. Those prototypes evolved directly from Model 30 No. 3 with an open lattice-work tail boom and one-piece cockpit enclosures. Later models had covered tail booms and open or two-piece cockpit enclosures. As the series progressed, Bell reverted to the open tail boom and one-piece cockpit bubble.

The basic Model 47 arrangement was a two or three-place side-by-side aircraft powered by a six cylinder, opposed, air-cooled engine. The engine was mounted vertically behind the cabin and drove a main and tail rotor by means of a two-stage, planetary, reduction-geared transmission, which was bolted to the engine, making the complete assembly one rigid unit. Bell's patented stabilizer bar was located below and at right angles to the two-blade main rotor. All models through the 47G/H-13G had laminated wooden rotor blades with a steel leading edge. The H-13H

and all subsequent models were equipped with bonded metal blades (most earlier types were retrofitted with the metal blades). The center section, to the rear of the cabin, was of welded tubular steel construction and supported the engine and tail boom. The tail boom was of similar construction, and supported the tail rotor drive shaft, variable-pitch tail rotor, ventral fin and elevator. A tail skid later gave way to a tail rotor guard which prevented damage during tail low landings.

It was possible to equip the helicopter with a variety of landing gear including, skids, floats, or quadracycle wheel landing gear. Bell pioneered skid landing gear for helicopters which were comprised of tubular skids attached to legs and straight (later arched) cross tubes, which, in turn, attached to the fuselage. When the CAA granted Bell the first NC license for float-equipped helicopters on 5 October 1946, it was expected that the Model 47 would be used in Canadian bush country for geophysical survey work. Float landing gear added about sixty pounds

Bell's chief test pilot, Floyd Carlson, gives Larry Bell a ride in the Model 30 No. 3 at Bell's Niagara Falls plant during 1945. (Bell)

5

One of the first twelve HTL-2s ordered by the Navy during 1948. The HTL featured Bell's split canopy for fair weather and special use. The doors were removed and the bubble's upper half replaced by a windshield visor. (Bell)

to the aircraft and consisted of sectional air-filled bags that could be installed only on straight cross tubes. The quadracycle landing gear consisted of four wheels attached to two cross tubes. The front wheels were self-castering, while the rear wheels of later models had parking brakes.

On 8 March 1946, the Model 47 was awarded the world's first commercial license followed by the first commercial delivery in December, which was concurrent with the first military sale to the U.S. Army. During April of 1947, thirteen Model 47s were delivered to the Air Force (YR-13) and Navy (HTL). The military Model 47 was later des-

Chief pilot Floyd Carlson demonstrates the stability of the Model 47 on 8 March 1946, the day Bell was awarded the first commercial helicopter license issued in the United States. (Bell)

ignated H-13, while the Army added the name Sioux, in keeping with their tradition of naming aircraft after American Indian tribes.

The Sioux was used for observation, utility, medical evacuation, and training. It saw extensive use in Korea, where it proved the value of the light helicopter, a lesson that would be repeated in Vietnam. During 1951, Bell moved its helicopter operations to Fort Worth, Texas, where more milestones were set. On 10 April 1953, the 1,000th Model 47 rolled off the assembly line. Near the end of the Korean hostilities, Larry Bell ordered full exploitation of the Model 47 for commercial use to prove the usefulness of the helicopter in peacetime.

Throughout its career, the Model 47 set records, highlighted in 1961 when Bell announced a new high altitude capability in the turbosupercharged Model 47G-3. Production flourished with each variant continually being upgraded. The 47J Ranger series was the only model to depart significantly from the basic 47. A total of 2,600 commercial and 2,400 military versions were built during a twenty-seven year production run which ended in 1973. By that time, more than twenty basic configurations had been produced with variants also built under license in Japan, Italy and England. Bell applied the experience it gained with the Model 47 to its UH-1 Huey series which was probably the only helicopter to exceed the Model 47 in worldwide popularity. The Model 47 proved a concept which set the trend for the future of helicopter development.

Development

H-13B/HTL-2

H-13C/D/E

H-13H

H-13J/HUL-1

HTL-5

HTL-7

OH-13S

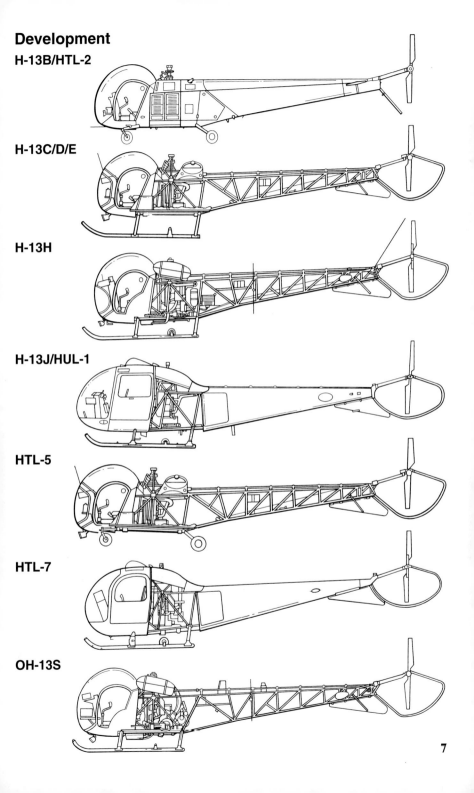

7

Production

The basic airframe of the H-13 series differed very little from model to model. The improvements/changes that were made to the aircraft being mostly to the landing gear (wheels or skids), engines, cockpit layout, fuel tanks and fuselage covering. Other changes were mostly in the form of add-ons, such as armament systems, stretcher kits and float landing gear kits. H-13 production variants include:

YR-13/HTL-1: A total of twenty-eight YR-13s (later designated YH-13) were delivered to the U.S. Air Force during 1947. They were powered by the Franklin 0-335-1 engine. Ten were transferred to the U.S. Navy as HTL-1s, two being later passed to the U.S. Coast Guard. The YR-13 had two seats, cruised at 80 mph, and fully loaded, could carry 2,100 pounds. Three Air Force machines were modified as YR-13As for cold-weather operations in Alaska.

H-13B/HTL-2: During 1948, the Army ordered sixty-five H-13Bs which were powered by the 200 hp Franklin 0-335-3 engine. The Navy ordered twelve of the type as HTL-2s. That model had changes made to the engine cowling, a two-piece "convertible" canopy was used, and the elevators were usually removed. The two-seat H-13B had a maximum weight of 2,200 pounds and could cruise at 85 mph.

H-13C: An H-13B was modified in 1950, by the removal of the fuselage covering and with skids installed to replace the wheeled landing gear. After successful tests, fifteen H-13Bs were converted during 1952 and fitted with two external litters.

H-13D/HTL-3,4: Skid landing gear was standard on eighty-seven aircraft delivered to the Army, while Navy HTLs were equipped with wheels or skids. Nine HTL-3s were delivered before introduction of the HTL-4, which featured an improved transmission. Dual controls became optional with this variant and a larger cockpit bubble enclosed a three-seat cockpit. The H-13D introduced the tail rotor guard and ventral fin.

H-13E/HTL-5: The individual seats of previous models were changed to a three position bench seat in the H-13E. Other changes included an improved transmission and engine, plus dual controls. The Army procured 490 H-13Es and the Navy bought thirty-six HTL-5s. They were redesignated OH-

A HTL-1 of Utility Helicopter Squadron One (HU-1) is chocked on the deck of a Navy icebreaker off Alaska during late 1950. (via Ned Gilliand)

Fuselage Development

H-13B/HTL-2

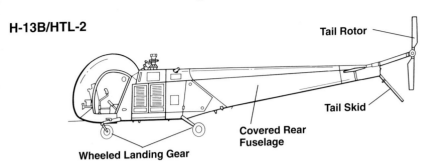

Tail Rotor

Tail Skid

Covered Rear Fuselage

Wheeled Landing Gear

H-13C/D/E, HTL-3/4/5

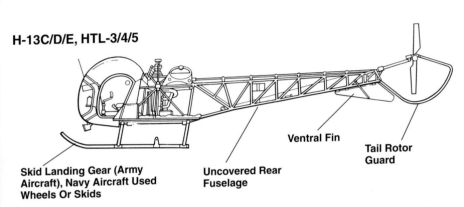

Ventral Fin

Tail Rotor Guard

Skid Landing Gear (Army Aircraft), Navy Aircraft Used Wheels Or Skids

Uncovered Rear Fuselage

Structural and engine components form a maze on this H-13E at the Army Aviation Museum at Fort Rucker, Alabama. The small oval fuel tank design was replaced by a larger type on later H-13s. (Keith Lovern)

This OH-13E was among a few transferred to the Air Force. Number 51-13809 was assigned to the USAF Flight Test Center at Edwards Air Force Base during early 1969. (Norm Taylor)

Float Kit

Any H-13 Variant Could Be Fitted With A Dual FLoat Kit

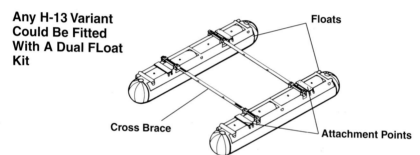

Floats

Cross Brace

Attachment Points

BuNo 122461 was one of two HTL-1s transferred from the Navy to the Coast Guard at Elizabeth City Air Station, North Carolina, during 1947. The aircraft originally was fitted with a wheeled landing gear, but was modified with floats and engine shields and shrouds to protect electronic gear mounted in the tail boom's open lattice frame. (via Ned Gilliand)

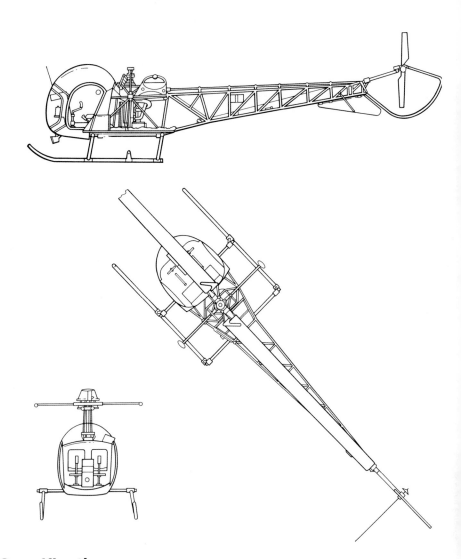

Specification

Bell OH-13E

Rotor Diameter.....35 feet 1 inch (10.7 m)
Length...................27 feet 4 inches (8.38 m)
Height....................9 feet 6 inches (2.89 m)
Empty Weight.......1,730 pounds (784.7 kg)
Maximum Weight..2,500pounds (1,134 kg)

Speed..................85mph (136.7kph)
Service Ceiling...13,000 feet (3,962.4 m)
Range..................200 miles (321.86 km)
Crew....................Two or three

Powerplant............One 220 hp Franlkin O-335-5 air-cooled engine.
Armament...............Normally none, although various armament kits could be carried.

Bell's chief test pilot R.C. Buyers conducts a test flight in a new production HTL-4 at the Bell plant in Fort Worth, Texas, during 1951. Navy aircraft could be fitted with either wheel or skid landing gear. (via Ned Giliand)

13E and TH-13L during 1962.

H-13G/HTL-6: Dual forty-three gallon fuel tanks were introduced on the H-13G along with an enlarged cockpit and bubble. A synchronized elevator improved stability and increased the center-of-gravity range. Power was upgraded with the installation of the 200 hp Lycoming VO-435, permitting a maximum weight of 2,350 pounds and a top speed of 90 mph. The Navy took delivery of forty-eight HTL-6 training versions which were equipped with new rotor brakes. Float kits were available for the type which became TH-13M in 1962. The Army ordered a total of 265 H-13Gs later redesignated as OH-13G.

H-13H: First ordered during 1955, H-13H production eventually totaled 470 aircraft. Powered by a 250 hp Lycoming VO-435-23, the type could cruise at 100 mph at a maximum weight of 2,450 pounds. The three-seat variant had a range of 240 miles and a service ceiling of 12,600 feet. Features included dual

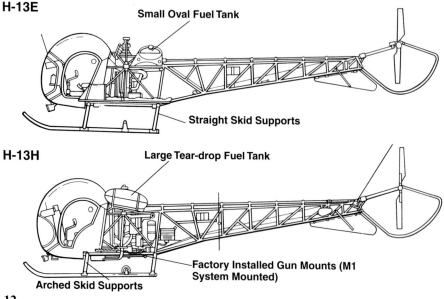

H-13E

Small Oval Fuel Tank

Straight Skid Supports

H-13H

Large Tear-drop Fuel Tank

Factory Installed Gun Mounts (M1 System Mounted)

Arched Skid Supports

This H-13H was transferred to the Navy where it was painted Blue, White, Red and Yellow for recruiting duties in the early 1980s. (Terry Love)

controls, dual radios, all-metal rotor blades, and arched skid cross tubes. The H-13H was the first Sioux to have factory-installed machine gun mounts. A few were transferred to the Air Force as UH-13Hs during 1962, when Army machines became OH-13Hs.

HTL-7: The Navy ordered eighteen of the type into production during 1957 as a primary and instrument trainer. Although built with the HUL-1 airframe, the HTL-7's two-seat cockpit incorporated all-weather instruments and dual controls. Two machines were used by the U.S. Coast Guard aboard ice-breakers. During 1962, they were redesignated TH-13Ns.

H-13J/HUL-1: Powered by a 240 hp Lycoming VO-435-21, the H-13J could accommodate four persons; the pilot in front and three passengers on a bench seat (which was removable to make room for two stretchers). A number of Navy versions had an electric winch installed for rescue work. Most

Prior to February of 1955, most Navy helicopters were painted Gloss Sea Blue, like this HUL-1 assigned to Naval Air Station Panama City. BuNo 143143 was part of the second batch of HUL-1s delivered to the Navy. (Terry Love)

This was the fifth-built OH-13S (s/n 639076) to come off the assembly line. It became a common practice to paint the upper portion of the cockpit bubble with White paint or shoe polish to minimize the sun's heat and prevent vertigo from the rotor blades. (USAF)

were fully covered for streamlining with the exception of military types flown in hot climates, which were operated without panels for engine cooling. Two were customized for use by President Eisenhower and operated under Air Force control. The Navy procured twenty-eight HUL-1s, which were powered by the 260 hp Lycoming VO-435-B1B. A pair were transferred to the Coast Guard as HUL-1Gs, which were redesignated HH-13Qs in 1962. The Presidential duo later became UH-13Js.

H-13H

Two Or Three Seat Cockpit

Open Frame Fuselage

H-13J/HUL-1

Four Seat Cabin

Enclosed Fuselage

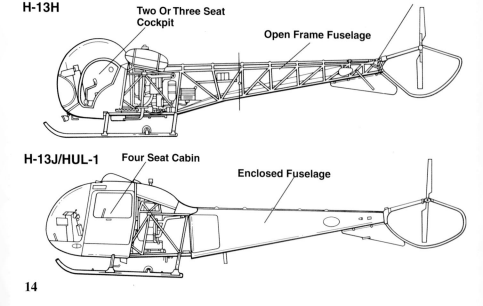

This was one of the two H-13J/VH-13Js customized for use by President Eisenhower during 1957. The pair were painted Blue and White and redesignated as UH-13Js during 1962. (Bell)

H-13K: Built during 1959, a pair of H-13Hs were re-engined during 1960 with a turbocharged 225 hp Franklin engine and a larger diameter rotor for high altitude performance. They were used by the Army and went on to establish two women's records for altitude and non-stop distance in 1961.

OH-13S: Built as a successor to the Army's OH-13H, the three-seat OH-13S was powered by a 260 hp turbo-supercharged Lycoming TV0-435-25 engine. The tail boom was lengthened by fourteen inches, the rotor blades were one foot longer, and gross weight increased to 2,850 pounds. Deliveries began during 1961, totaling 265 aircraft. The "Ultimate S" cruised at 90 mph and had a range of 325 miles.

TH-13T: Basically similar to the OH-13S, the two-seat trainer's cabin was eight inches wider, had a tinted cockpit bubble, and featured additional avionics and a blind flying hood. Added power was derived from a 270 hp Lycoming engine. The Army placed an initial order for 103 examples in 1964 with production eventually totaling 411 TH-13Ts.

An OH-13S awaiting delivery on the ramp at Bell's Fort Worth, Texas plant during 1964. White polish was added to the top of the cockpit bubble and a shield mounted forward of the anti-collision light on top of the tail boom prevented glare from the light from interfering with the pilot. (Bell)

Operational Service

The U.S. Navy, in its search for a suitable rotary-wing trainer, awarded the initial HTL (Helicopter, Training, Light) contract to Bell on 20 June 1946, with the first aircraft being delivered in February of 1947. Helicopter Utility Squadron One (HU-1), the first of its type in the Navy, was commissioned on 1 April 1948. Exactly one year later HU-2 was formed, becoming the first Navy squadron with HTL aircraft assigned.

On 4 December 1950, the Navy established Helicopter Training Unit One (HTU-1) at Naval Air Station Ellyson Field, Pensacola, Florida. By late 1951, HTU-1 had nearly sixty helicopters on hand for training Navy and Marine Corps pilots and by the end of 1952, the unit had eight HTL-4s and thirty-four HTL-5s. The H-13 series remained the primary basic training helicopter at Ellyson until February of 1969.

The Navy accepted a total of 183 HTL aircraft beginning with the HTL-1, followed by successive models up to the HTL-7, the last of which was delivered in July of 1959. A total of thirty-four HUL (Helicopter, Utility, Light) variants were also procured by the Navy, the first of which arrived in November of 1955. The HUL became operational with HU-2 in January of 1957, and the following month was used for drone tests. Fitted with Mk 43 torpedoes, the HUL-1 demonstrated the feasibility of assigning torpedo-laden drone helicopters to destroyers. This led to the development of the Drone Anti-Sub Helicopters (DASH). Final delivery of the type took place in March of 1959, although Navy H-13 variants remained active on squadron rosters until June of 1973.

Marine helicopter aviation had its official beginning on 1 December 1947, when Helicopter Squadron One (HMX-1) was commissioned. Marine Corps interest in helicopters centered around the observation role; however, since no helicopters had been designed specifically for military observation, the Marines were hesitant to replace their fixed-wing observation aircraft. The Navy, which was procuring a number of HTLs, loaned an HTL-2 to HMX-1 in August of 1948. Marine leaders were sold on the idea when they found that the HTL was superior to fixed-wing aircraft in the observation role. During 1949, the Chief of Naval Operations (CNO) designated the Bell HTL as the primary observation aircraft for the Marine Corps.

The pair of Coast Guard HTL-1s were replaced by two HUL-1Gs during 1959. This HUL-1G, Number 1337, was conducting a test flight at the Bell factory prior to delivery in 1958. The aircraft was later fitted with floats for ice-breaker duty in the Gulf of Alaska. (Bell)

A Coast Guard HTL-4 passes close to Miss Liberty during a harbor patrol flight on 3 December 1952. The Coast Guard helicopter operated under the Port of New York Captain and was responsible for port security, which included; searching for polluters, smugglers, illegal dumping, and for search and rescue duties. The aircraft was based at Floyd Bennett Field. (U.S. Coast Guard)

This HTL-5 was among the last of thirty-six aircraft ordered by the Navy. These aircraft were redesignated as TH-13Ls when the Navy changed its designation system during 1962. (Bell)

By 1 July of that year, HMX-1 had two HTLs, followed by two more one year later. Helicopter Observation Squadron Six (VMO-6), which was attached to the 1st Marine Division and sent to Korea, received twelve HTLs. Due to a critical helicopter shortage in the war zone, ten Navy HTL-4s were turned over to VMO-6. Meanwhile, VMO-1 acquired HTLs in September of 1951, and VMO-2 received theirs in July.

Marine helicopter pilots received their training at NAS Ellyson Field in Navy H-13s until 1967, when a severe pilot shortage, caused by the buildup of the Vietnam war, pushed additional pilots into the Army training syllabus which included H-13s.

The Army received authorization for organic aircraft in June of 1942, and, by late 1945, had reached a tentative agreement with the Air Corps for some Army pilots to be trained

A HTL-6 in the final rework stage at Naval Air Station Jacksonville's Overhaul & Repair Department during June of 1966. This aircraft is finished in the standard USN HTL training scheme of overall International Orange, with Yellow tail components, and Dark Gray skids and engine support framework. (Ron Williamson)

Rotor Head

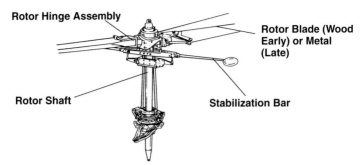

Rotor Hinge Assembly

Rotor Blade (Wood Early) or Metal (Late)

Rotor Shaft

Stabilization Bar

as helicopter pilots. By 1947, a pact led to the first helicopter pilot training class in September at San Marcos, Texas using H-13s. Since then and the beginning of the Korean war, Army aircraft procurement had barely any perceptible momentum. That changed drastically in 1951, when annual aircraft appropriation funds jumped from $2 million to $42 million dollars. When war broke out, the Army had sixty-three H-13s, which sky-rocketed to more than 600 by December of 1954, six months after the armistice. During the war, Army helicopters not only transport-ed troops and supplies, but became flying ambulances. Field demands for them grew, prompting the Army to request some 3,000 helicopters.

When four H-13s arrived at Saigon, Vietnam's port, in late 1961 and flew their first combat mission on 2 January 1962, they officially ushered in "the helicopter war." At that time the Army air fleet consisted of 5,600 aircraft, of which almost half were heli-copters. The H-13 accounted for one third that number, with 285 OH-13E, 185 OH-13G, and 391 OH-13H Models. The H-13 had left Vietnam by late 1969 and by March of 1970, when the Army aircraft inventory in Vietnam peaked, only one OH-13S remained. Meanwhile, the worldwide Army inventory held 203 OH-13Es, 148 OH-13Gs, 285 OH-13Hs, 71 OH-13Ss, and 398 TH-13Ts. The following year, 179 OH-13s in Europe were deemed excess and most of them earmarked for foreign military sales. During 1972, the majority of H-13s were passed to the Reserves, where the type was replaced by OH-6As and OH-58s by 1976.

A few Navy HTL-6s were used for astronaut training during the 1960s. This aircraft was preserved and is now displayed at the National Museum of Naval Aviation, Pensacola, Florida. (U.S. Navy)

An Army Helicopter Flight Demonstration Team OH-13H practices its clown show routine with an empty drum for one of the many team demonstrations held in Europe during 1961 and 1962. (Bell)

A total of eight military Bell HTL series helicopters were used by the U.S. Coast Guard for a wide variety of duties. Beginning in May of 1947, the service received a HTL-1 from the Navy which had ordered an initial batch of ten aircraft. Although originally a U.S. Army Air Force YH-13 (serial 46-253), the machine was assigned a Navy Bureau Number (BuNo 122460). The last HTL-1 from the Navy order was transferred to the Coast Guard in June of 1947 with BuNo 122461 (ex USAAF 46-254). Both aircraft operated under the Port of New York Captain, to survey the harbor area, usually with floats attached, seeking out smugglers, saboteurs, maritime offenders, and harbor pollution. The first HTL-1 crashed in December of 1952 with the other being disposed of in 1955. That same year, a single HTL-4 (BuNo 128623) was transferred form the Navy. Fitted with float gear, the type was used for ice reconnaissance, search and rescue, and also operated from the cutter STORIS off Nome, Alaska during Distant Early Warning (DEW) line operations. For a time, the helicopter retained the USN bureau number and markings of HU-1.

Three HTL-5s were purchased by the Coast Guard and delivered in February of 1952. Assigned USCG serials 1268, 1269, and 1270, they were used for scouting passage through ice, and transporting personnel and cargo from ship to shore over ice-blocked areas. They also saw service with the USCG Port Security in New York, operating from Floyd Bennett Field, remaining in use until 1960.

Two four-place HUL-1s were transferred from the Navy in 1959 and redesignated HUL-1Gs in Coast Guard service. Both aircraft were assigned standard USCG four-digit serials, 1337 and 1338. In addition to full instrumentation for night flying, both machines featured a 400 pound capacity rescue hoist. Both flew ice reconnaissance from the icebreaker NORTHWIND during the 1959 Bering Sea Patrol, and later operated from the cutter STORIS in the Bering Sea for search and rescue and utility duty. One float-equipped aircraft operated from cutters and icebreakers in the Gulf of Alaska during the 1960s. The other was ski-equipped and operated from Kodiak Air Station, Alaska during the same period. The type was redesignated HH-13Q in 1962 and served the Coast Guard until December of 1967.

In August of 1962, two float-equipped Navy HTL-7s (BuNos 145848 and 145853) were loaned to the Coast Guard, one of which was assigned to cutters. The pair, redesignated TH-13Ns in 1962 and later HH-13Ns, served until October of 1968, and, two months later, were placed in storage at MASDC, Davis-Monthon AFB, Arizona.

Korea

By the late 1940s, the newly designed Bell Model 47 had displayed remarkable performance and reliability. It was quickly adopted by the armed forces for a number of roles, especially rescue and reconnaissance. War-torn Korea became the proving ground for the helicopter, since this war saw the first mass employment of rotary-wing aircraft.

The most dramatic and publicized use of helicopters in the campaign focused on the medical evacuation of combat casualties. Although Korea's geography precluded an adequate road system, the emerging helicopter could overcome this problem and easily negotiate the rugged terrain. Its speed, flexibility, and ability to provide patient comfort significantly shortened the time span between wound and surgery. Many casualties were so critically wounded that evacuation by any other means would have diminished any chance for survival. Eighty percent of all front-line evacuations in Korea were attributed to U.S. Army H-13s, as well as a smaller contingent of Marine Corps HTLs. The Army operated the H-13B, H-13C, H-13D and H-13E throughout the conflict, almost exclusively for medical evacuation. Most flew in direct support of three of the four Mobile Army Surgical Hospitals (MASH) units, with the fourth supported by U.S. Air Force helicopters. It was that setting which the popular M*A*S*H* TV series was based.

Due to an urgent shortage of helicopters in the Marine Corps brought on by the Korean war, ten Navy HTL-4s were turned over to Marine Squadron VMO-6. Besides medical evacuation, the Marines flew artillery spotting missions with their H-13s. The USMC HTLs eventually replaced the H03S-1, becoming the primary Marine medical evacuation helicopter. Army and Marine H-13s flew other missions which included resupply, reconnaissance, radio relay, and ship-to-shore transport.

The use of helicopters for medical evacuation had its origin in circumstance rather than planning. At the beginning of the Korean war, Detachment F of the USAF 3rd Air Rescue Squadron, which had been tasked primarily with downed pilot rescue, also received requests from ground elements for casualty evacuation. Many successful missions, derived from those requests, prompted the U.S Eighth Army to test its helicopters for similar duties. After a successful Joint Army/Air Force experiment at Taegu on 3 August 1950, the Army Surgeon General strived to obtain helicopters for medical evacuation within the Eighth Army. His efforts were rewarded on 22 November when the 2nd Helicopter Detachment arrived in Korea with four H-13s. Within one week of arrival, one of the unit's H-13Bs became the first Army helicopter flown into combat. However, the exact date was never recorded since the aircraft flew in support of Eighth Army units withdrawing from a major Chinese assault. After a period of in-country training, the unit became operational on 1 January 1951, and attached to the 8055th MASH at Anscom City. Two weeks later, as the Chinese continued to push Eighth Army elements back to Seoul, the first Army medical evacuation mission was flown in one of the H-13s. At the controls was Captain Albert Sebourn, who later designed an alternative patient litter for the H-13 in place of the standard stokes basket.

In January, the 3rd Detachment arrived with

A trio of 8th Army H-13Ds parked on the ramp of a Korean airfield during the Korean war. Eighth Army Sioux helicopters directly supported the Mobile Army Surgical Hospitals (MASH), flying wounded troops from the front lines to these units, greatly cutting down the time that it took to get a wounded man proper medical treatment. **(via Larry Davis)**

A wounded soldier is prepared for evacuation on the external litter attached to the skids of a H-13D. The aircraft was equipped with a cover over the engine, which was used in cold weather to make the engine easier to start. (US Army)

A H-13D assigned to a MASH unit lifts off from the Korean countryside with wounded aboard. The small ground handling wheels, normally attached to the skids, were usually removed from Korea-based H-13s. (US Army)

HTL-4s eventually replaced the HO3S-1 as the primary Marine Corps medevac helicopter in Korea. These were painted Gloss Sea Blue and carried a litter on each side of the aircraft. This HTL-4 was assigned to Marine Helicopter Squadron One (HMX-1). (National Archives)

four H-13s, followed by the 4th Detachment several days later, also with four Sioux. The 3rd became operational with the 8076th MASH and the 4th was assigned to 1st MASH. On 21 February 1951, the 1st Helicopter Detachment arrived in Korea with four H-13s and was attached to the Eighth Army Flight Detachment. Shortly after its arrival; however, it was stripped of its H-13s, which were passed on to other units. Eventually, all H-13Bs in the theater were replaced by H-13Ds.

So intense was the action that all four pilots of the 2nd Helicopter Detachment had been awarded the Distinguished Flying Cross, after only two weeks. During their first month of operations they evacuated more than 500 severely wounded, in one instance, twenty-three from a single location. They often flew supplies to besieged units, then flew the wounded out, earning the profound respect of their comrades.

Army H-13s that operated in cold weather climates had their engines enclosed in specially-made cold weather cowlings. The engine compartment of this H-13E in Korea was being pre-heated by ground crews, to make starting the engine easier. (Smithsonian Institution)

H-l3s performed admirably as the main observation and medical evacuation helicopter of the Korean conflict, teaching the U.S. Armed Services many of the lessions of helicopter operations that would become vital in a later war. This H-13D was modified with dual landing lights under the cockpit bubble. (Bell)

The four detachments were redesignated Army Units (AU) under the Eighth Army on 14 May 1951. The 1st Detachment was disbanded, while the remaining 2nd, 3rd and 4th became the 49th, 50th and 52nd Medical Detachment Helicopter Ambulance respectively, in December of 1952. Until June of 1953, when a fourth detachment was formed, the Surgeon General had only a dozen H-13s operating in Korea - four in each detachment.

Medical Detachment personnel made modifications to their H-13s to improve the care of their wounded passengers. Undetachable stokes baskets gave way to removable litters with Plexiglas covers. Thanks to GI ingenuity, the pods were heated with warm air piped from the engine manifold. Some aircraft had a plasma bottle holder mounted on the cabin exterior behind the door openings to facilitate blood replacement while airborne.

During the final months of hostilities, some H-13s were replaced by much larger H-19s, which did double duty as cargo and rescue helicopters. By the end of the war (27 July 1953) a total of 21,212 soldiers had been evacuated by helicopter. Some sources put the number closer to 25,000, considering civilian casualties and non-combat related injuries. The original H-13 pilots that served in Korea were not medical personnel but culled from other branches. During 1952, the Medical Corps began training its own pilots, who arrived in Korea shortly after the armistice but maintained an average of sixty medical missions per month throughout the country.

Extensive use of the H-13 and HTL in Korea accelerated the development of larger and more powerful helicopters. The lessons learned in medical evacuation during the Korean and Vietnam wars led to the development of civil medical evacuation by helicopter that is significant in saving lives today.

Rescue Litter

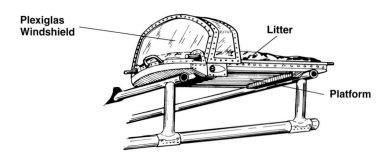

Plexiglas Windshield

Litter

Platform

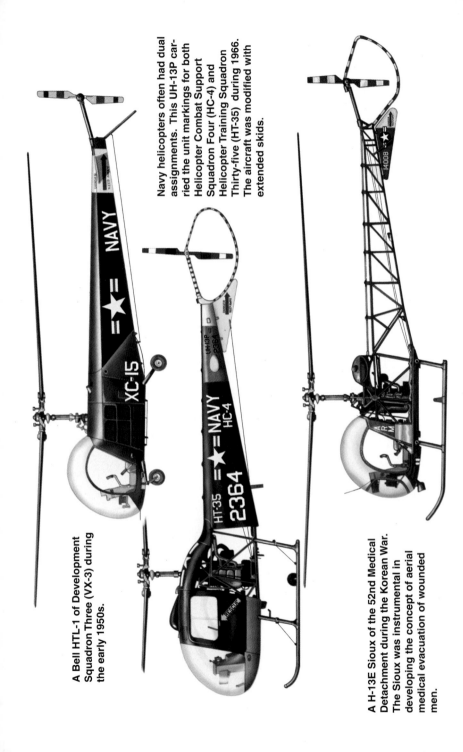

A Bell HTL-1 of Development Squadron Three (VX-3) during the early 1950s.

Navy helicopters often had dual assignments. This UH-13P carried the unit markings for both Helicopter Combat Support Squadron Four (HC-4) and Helicopter Training Squadron Thirty-five (HT-35) during 1966. The aircraft was modified with extended skids.

A H-13E Sioux of the 52nd Medical Detachment during the Korean War. The Sioux was instrumental in developing the concept of aerial medical evacuation of wounded men.

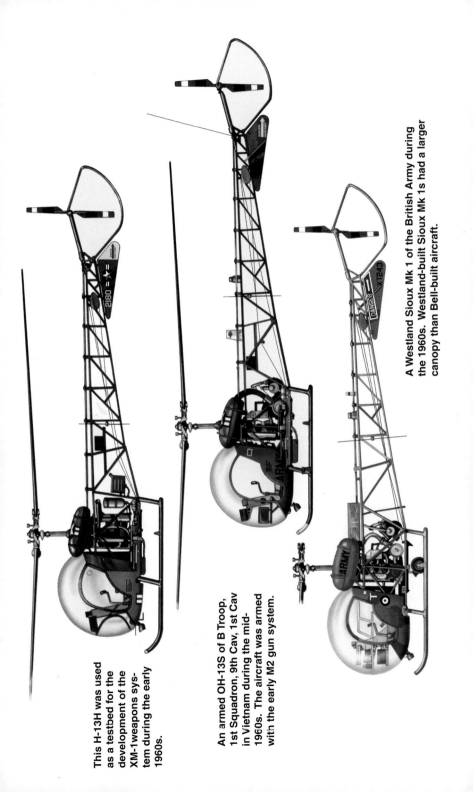

This H-13H was used as a testbed for the development of the XM-1 weapons system during the early 1960s.

An armed OH-13S of B Troop, 1st Squadron, 9th Cav, 1st Cav in Vietnam during the mid-1960s. The aircraft was armed with the early M2 gun system.

A Westland Sioux Mk 1 of the British Army during the 1960s. Westland-built Sioux Mk 1s had a larger canopy than Bell-built aircraft.

Sioux Warrior

The H-13 underwent extensive testing as a weapons platform and was instrumental in the development of a number of helicopter armament systems. Although labeled an observation aircraft and docile in appearance, the armed Sioux proved to be a formidable attack aircraft in the hands of air cavalry units in Vietnam.

The Army began experimenting with weapons systems for the H-13 as early as 1953, while it was still flying medical evacuation missions during the final days of the Korean War. That deviation from humanitarian service began in earnest during the late 1950s when the Army Aviation Center's, Combat Development Office worked diligently to develop an armed helicopter strike force. Despite severe opposition from senior Army officials and the Air Force (who seemed to view anything Army aviation did as an infringement into their territory), the Army persevered and formed a unit to serve as a test bed for their ideas. The 7292nd Aerial Combat Reconnaissance Company (ACR) began life at Tiger Port, Fort Rucker, Alabama on 24 March 1958. The unit experimented with numerous helicopter weapons systems, many of which were locally fabricated by ACR personnel and, if found useful, were standardized by late 1959. The ACR was later redesignated 8305th ACR, evolving into the Aerial Reconnaissance and Security Troop during 1959, and, finally, became the genesis of the famed air cavalry.

The ACR employed a mix of H-13Ds, H-13Es, and H-13Hs, for a myriad of weapons tests that lasted until 1963. Heavier weapons adopted for other helicopters were denied the H-13 due to insufficient power and subsequent weight restrictions.

Among the first systems tested on the Sioux was the XM1 which became the first standardized kit for scout aircraft. The XM-1 system utilized the Browning M37C .30 caliber air cooled machine gun (normally mounted on tanks). Later, this system was modified with the M60C 7.62MM machine gun and redesignated as the M2. Other early variations of the M1 used up to eight .30 caliber guns coupled with rocket combinations from single to ten-cell units. Those kits typically featured an arrangement of guns mounted on top of each skid, with the rockets fastened underneath. Even with minimal ammunition loads, those systems proved too heavy for the H-13 and were discarded in favor of

During the initial stages of armed helicopter development, an H-13 was secured to a wooden platform at the Matteson Range, Fort Rucker, Alabama, and used to test a number of different armament systems. For this test, the aircraft was fitted with an ACR rocket kit "L" during September of 1957. (US Army)

This H-13 was outfitted with a pair of Swiss-made Oerlikon rockets and a pair of .30 caliber machine guns. (US Army)

This experimental ACR kit was comprised of a pair of Aerial AN-M2 .30 caliber machine guns plus a six-tube cell of 2.75 inch Folding Fin Aerial Rockets (FFAR). The aircraft was based at Fort Rucker during the 1950s, and had the small ground handling wheels relocated to accommodate the machine gun drum magazines. (US Army)

This unusual armament system combined a pair of infantry-type M60 machine guns and eight experimental anti-tank rockets developed by the Redstone Arsenal. The supply of rockets was exhausted by the time the kit was operational, so it was modified to accept standard 2.75 inch FFAR rockets. Only the center four tubes were functional since the outboard tubes did not clear the gun barrels. This kit was designed by General Electric for exclusive use on helicopters. This, and other systems tested on H-13s, hung so low that they were often damaged when the aircraft landed on rough surfaces. (US Army)

the lighter M2 system.

Although the Army placed a high priority upon defensive helicopter armament due to an urgent operational requirement, they considered the M2 only minimally satisfactory, yet it became the standard for OH-13S (and OH-23G) scout helicopters during the first two years of Vietnam operations. The forward-firing M2 system was comprised of a M60C machine gun mounted on top of each skid, and, like most early weapons systems, it was sighted by grease pencil marks on the

This was a Bell-manufactured napalm canister that was tested on H-13s at Fort Bragg during 1962. (US Army)

A makeshift Bazooka mount was fitted to this H-I3D during 1950. The mount held a standard infantry Bazooka rocket launcher and became the first tube weapon fired from a Bell helicopter. (Bell)

cockpit glass. Later, a ring and optical sight was added. In combat, the kit was plagued by recharging problems and Vietnam's high density altitude, which prompted most units to remove one gun, often replacing it with a small rocket system. Eventually, the entire kit was eliminated to improve aircraft performance. The system weighed just over 200

This Redstone design used extra long rocket tubes to test dispersion patterns. It was found that longer tubes did not result in a more concentrated pattern and the ACR kit was not adopted as standard. The weapon system also mounted a single .30 cal. machine gun carried above the tubes on each side. (Bell)

This makeshift grenade launcher was tested on a H-13 by the 24th Infantry Division in Japan during early 1953. (US Army)

pounds, carried 1,100 rounds of ammunition, and had a maximum effective range of 1,000 meters.

A wide variety of rocket systems were also tested, often in combination with machine guns. Swiss-manufactured Oerlikon rockets were available as leftovers from a program whose funding never materialized. The French SS-10 wire-guided missile was included in the tests, having been introduced into the Army during 1959. The SS-10 (later SS-11) was given the Army designation AGM-22B and saw limited use in Vietnam on Huey gunships.

Fixed heavy weapons finally gave way to a door gun system utilizing the 7.62MM M60A machine gun operated by an observer. The gun was initially positioned on top of a swing-out Sagami mount attached to the right skid. A 200 round ammunition box was attached to the weapon's feed mechanism. To reduce its size and weight, scout crews later removed the barrel flash suppressor, sights, bipod, and, in some cases, the shoulder stock. When hung from a bungee cord in the doorway and fed from a large ammo box on the floor, observers found that the stripped down gun afforded them a great deal of latitude. An ample supply of various grenades and individual weapons filled out the scout observer's arsenal.

As early as 1951, Marine Corps Squadron HMX-1 had experimented with mounting machine guns and 2.75 inch rockets on their HTL-4s; however, there was little interest in developing the helicopter for close support. In addition, many Korean war pilots with combat experience were against the concept. Ultimately, the limited number of Marine helicopters dispelled the idea of procuring rotary-wing aircraft as a substitute for close support fixed-wing aircraft.

A H-13H, assigned to the US Army Ordnance Plant at Mainz, Germany during 1959, carries two underslung .30 caliber machine guns. The box mounted under the fuselage was the ammunition supply for the two guns. (National Archives)

31

A pair of .30 caliber M37C machine guns were attached to the skid cross tubes on this H-13K at Aberdeen Proving Ground. This was a non-standard mounting that proved impractical. (National Archives)

M37 .30 Caliber Machine Gun (M1 System)

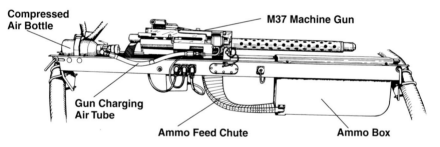

Compressed Air Bottle

M37 Machine Gun

Gun Charging Air Tube

Ammo Feed Chute

Ammo Box

The XM-1 dual-gun system was mounted on the skids of a H-13H during late 1963. This armament kit used coaxial M37 .30 caliber tank machine guns and became the first standardized system, being known as the M1. (US Army)

This H-13E carried a standard M60A 7.62ᴍᴍ machine gun affixed to the skid cross tubes on each side. When the M60 replaced the M37 .30 caliber machine gun as the standard weapon in the M1 system, the system was redesignated the M2 system. (US Army)

M60 Machine Gun

The ultimate tank buster! The French SS-10 anti-tank rocket came to Fort Rucker during 1960 and, like any other weapon, was eventually strapped to an H-13. The test aircraft, in this case, was a H-I3H of the Aviation Board. (US Army)

33

Vietnam

When observation helicopters were introduced into the Vietnam conflict, the Army air fleet had 861 H-13Es, OH-13Gs and OH-13Hs. The first helicopters sent for direct support of South Vietnamese government forces and the U.S. Military Advisory Group arrived in Saigon in December of 1961. The 8th and 57th Transportation Companies were deployed, each with twenty CH-21 Shawnee troop carriers and two OH-13Es. Although the H-13s returned to the U.S. with a minimum of combat exposure, the type was reintroduced into Vietnam during 1962, attached to CH-21 units. As the Army's primary observation helicopter during the early war years, the Sioux quickly proved the importance and effectiveness of reconnaissance, since these flights actually stirred the enemy into combat. During the first two years of airmobile operations, scout helicopters flew more than 500,000 sorties during which twenty-five OH-13s and 0H-23s were lost.

The air cavalry troop was one of the basic unit structures upon which the airmobile concept was built. The predecessor of the first air cavalry troop was the 11th Air Assault Division (AAD), initially assigned nine H-13S scouts, which was formed during 1963. The 11th AAD evolved into the famed 1st Cavalry Division (officially redesignated 3 July 1965), which became the first major unit designed specifically for airmobile operations. The division took on two additional air cav troops, plus a ground troop, which formed the 1st Squadron/9th Cavalry, better known as 1/9. In addition to the nine or ten OH-13S scouts assigned each air cav troop, thirty-four OH-13s were culled from other units for distribution to other levels within the 1st Cav. Boasting a fleet of 428 helicopters (sixty-four of them OH-13S scouts), the 1st Cav sailed to Vietnam aboard carriers, arriving on 15 September1965.

The 1/9 became legendary, having been credited with initiating more then half of the 1st Cav's enemy contacts. The OH-13 crews of that unit discovered the hiding places of the North Vietnamese Army's 32nd, 33rd and 66th Regiments, resulting in first blood at the battle of Ia Drang. A variety of other Army units in Vietnam also utilized the OH-13s, primarily in the scout role.

While developing the airmobile concept, Army commanders refined tactics by experimenting with a variety of combinations of helicopters. The function of those teams were designated by the colors Blue, Red, White

An OH-13S of the Ist Cavalry Division undergoes extensive maintenance on the PSP ramp of an Army base in Vietnam's central highlands. Both fuel tanks have been removed and are on the ramp behind the aircraft. (Ron Woodman via Lennart Lundh)

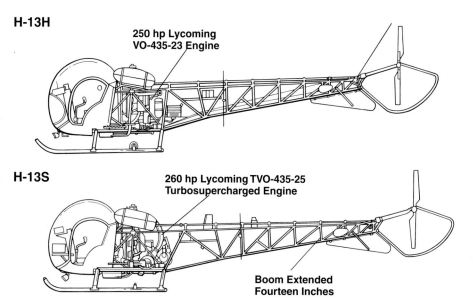

H-13H

250 hp Lycoming
VO-435-23 Engine

H-13S

260 hp Lycoming TVO-435-25
Turbosupercharged Engine

Boom Extended
Fourteen Inches

and Pink. Basically, all were comprised of two choppers, except the Blue, which was the UH-I Huey element that carried the ground troops. Red identified a pair of gunships, while White was solely reconnaissance. The blending of the two colors, or one gunship and one observation helicopter, formed a Pink Team which had more flexibility.

The Pink team became the most common tactical combination used by the air cav. As the White element of the Pink Team, the OH-13 flew low and slow searching for the elusive enemy, often purposely trying to draw fire, giving the orbiting gunship a target.

Quick reflexes and skill were the name of the game to ensure the gunships were rolling

This badly damaged OH-13S of the 1st Cav was cannibalized for spare parts to keep other Sioux scouts flying. The OH-13S was the primary H-13 variant used in Vietnam. (Melvin Edwards)

The observer's position of a Vietnam-based OH-13S Scout. An M60A machine gun rests in the open doorway, while smoke and phosphorous grenades are strung outside the door in easy reach. The M2 gun system mount attached to the skid cross tubes was empty. This mount would normally carry a M60 machine gun; however, the weight of the system led many units to discard the system in favor of a flexible door gun. (Melvin Edwards)

onto the target, even before the scout ship was clear. The observer/gunner aboard the scout helicopter was relied upon to eliminate any lapse of coverage, and a second gunship was often added for increased firepower. A Pink Team worked in concert with a flight of Blues (Aero Rifle Platoon), providing reconnaissance and gun support. When supporting Blues as a White Team, a lone OH-13 flew at (or below) tree top level in search of enemy positions, while the other flew high, to provide cover fire, radio relay, and, rescue, if the

An OH-13S Scout of B Troop, 1/9 Cavalry, 1st Air Cavalry Division. The Red dirt strip identifies this as a forward base in Vietnam's northern region. (Melvin Edwards)

Sandbagged revetments were used to protect 1st Cav OH-13S Scouts after a number of aircraft were destroyed by enemy mortar attacks. (Melvin Edwards)

low bird went down.

Scout missions were nothing short of high risk; fourteen of the original twenty pilots of 1/9 were killed in less than six months. Not only did the helicopters fly slow through the trees to find the enemy and draw fire but, returned to the dangerous environment to survey the battle damage from their fire. Because of their incredibly hazardous missions, scout aircrews became legendary and were often characterized as daring bawdy maniacs.

Most air cav units that deployed to Vietnam during the early war years were equipped with the OH-13S. In 1967, the Army determined it required 377 light observation helicopters to adequately conduct operations in Vietnam. Since in-country aircraft availability fell short of that number, seventy-one OH-13s were moved from Europe to Vietnam during May 1967. By the end of August, 171 OH-13S scouts were sharing the scout role

An OH-13S of the 1st Cav takes its place among damaged Bell Hueys after a hard landing during 1969. The aircraft was a total loss and ended up being used as a source of spare parts for other Sioux Scouts. (George Sullivan)

37

A OH-13S Sioux of B Troop, 1/9th Cavalry, 1st Air Cavalry Division, makes an approach to a landing zone in Vietnam's central highlands during the mid 1960s. It was armed with a M2 weapons systems which is visible above the skids. (Melvin Edwards)

with 190 OH-23 Raven helicopters. By June of 1968, all OH-13s in Vietnam were slated for replacement by Hughes OH-6A Cayuse Light Observation Helicopters (LOH), the first of which arrived in October of 1967.

During the changeover period, the Army took delivery of 151 OH-13s to replace those lost in combat and as the result of accidents.

From an operational standpoint, the H-13 experienced severe limitations while operat-

This OH-13S was heavily damaged by an enemy attack on the 1st Air Cavalry Division's "Golf Course" airfield at An Khe, South Vietnam during early September of 1966. (US Army)

Armed with the M2 gun system, a OH-I3S of the 1st Cavalry cranks up for a mission in its revetment in the An Lao Valley during the Fall of 1967. (National Archives)

ing in Vietnam's high density altitude. The combination of hot climate and high altitude (especially in the central highlands), greatly reduced the lifting capability of the H-13. The tactical necessity to carry weapons and protective gear often cut lift to the extent that "running takeoffs" became commonplace. The two-fold solution to the problem was to lighten the aircraft and maintain airspeed to avoid the loss of transitional lift. On the plus side, the Sioux was difficult for enemy gunners to hit since they had become accustomed to "leading" faster aircraft. Aircrews also favored the ample room in the cockpit for ammo and other vital gear.

While not intended as a warship, H-13s in Vietnam were initially fitted with a variety of fixed weapons combinations. Those included skid-mounted M2 weapons systems, comprising two M60C machine guns (single and two-gun systems), M60A machine guns on Sagami mounts outside the observer's door, and 2.75 inch rocket pods. Since the total weight of the twin M60C system exceeded 200 pounds, first one, then both guns were discarded to improve performance. Rocket pods eventually gave way to hand-held M60A machine guns and a supply of fragmentation grenades for the observer. Armor vests and armor plating, usually scavenged from downed aircraft, were often placed under and behind seat cushions, or in the lower cockpit bubble for added protection.

Despite many mechanical problems, air-crews found the H-13 a most forgiving aircraft. Tales abound of H-13s taking numerous .30 caliber hits, yet bringing the crew safely home. H-13s were phased out of Vietnam by late 1969; however, due to dramatic OH-6A losses, a number were redeployed in January of 1971, only to be phased out again later that year. A total of seventy U.S. Army OH-13s were lost in Vietnam.

Although Vietnamese Air Force (VNAF) H-13 operations were limited, a few examples found their way into the allied air arm in 1956 as part of the 1st Helicopter Squadron at Tan Son Nhut Air Base. Additionally, some were used to form the 2nd Helicopter Squadron at Danang during 1961. Besides two Bell 47G Models acquired from the U.S. in 1960, it's believed that the VNAF also obtained a number of early models from the French.

Besides the American and VNAF H-13 assets in Vietnam, the Royal Australian Air Force (RAAF) operated Independent Reconnaissance Flight 161 with H-13Gs, nicknamed Possums. The unit performed a variety of duties including scouting for armor units, command and control, radio relay, resupply, medevac, and artillery adjustment.

Superseded by more maneuverable turbine-powered scout helicopters, little credit has been given the H-13's significant role in the development of air cavalry tactics or the service it rendered during the Vietnam conflict.

39

In Foreign Service

By 1950, Bell Helicopter had established itself on a global scale, gaining popularity with its Model 47. An early customer for the Model 47 was Canada, which took delivery of a Model 47B-3 in March of 1947. This was Bell's fifth production machine and it was used for spray work and later chartered by the Canadian government for evaluation. On 1 September 1950, the Royal Canadian Navy formed its first helicopter unit with Model 47s. Eventually, the Royal Canadian Air Force acquired nine H-13s, all assigned to the Joint Air Training Command School.

Beginning in 1954, the Model 47 was built under license in Italy by Agusta. Specific models included the 47J-3 Super Ranger ASW version for the Italian Navy, which evolved from the Model 47J-2, with a modified transmission, new instruments, high efficiency rotor brake, and a single Mk 44 torpedo. Agusta also built the high altitude Model 47J-3B-1s for the Italian Air Force along with Models 47G, 47G-2, 47G-4A, 47G-5 and 47J. In mid-1961, Agusta produced an experimental variant called the A 115 which incorporated a Model 47J cabin, 47G rotor, tail boom, transmission and undercarriage, plus a Turbomeca Aztazou II 320 shp turbine

engine. A total of 1,200 Model 47 types were produced by Agusta before production ceased in 1976.

In the United Kingdom, the Model 47 was built under license by Westland, which retained the Sioux label. A total of 422 Westland Sioux were produced, 253 examples as Model 47G-3B-I for the British Army, which were redesignated AH Mk 1s. Other variants were the AT Mk 1 and Mk 2, which was dual control. Westland Sioux production began in March of 1965, and the last machine was delivered in December of 1969.

The Model 47 was also built under license by Kawasaki in Japan as the KH-4 (derived from Bell's Model 47G-3B). The modification resulted in a four-seat general purpose aircraft with a newly designed cabin enclosure, increased fuel capacity, altered control system, and redesigned instrument arrangement. An experimental version of the KH-4 was the KHR-1 flown in April 1968 to test a three-bladed rigid rotor system. Kawasaki also produced 180 Model 47G-2s, seventy-five of which went to the JGSDF. In addition, thirty-three Model 47G-2As were built, eight of which went to the JMSDF.

One major foreign customer was Spain, which operated a total of fifty-six Model 47s for its Army, Air Force and Navy from 1954 to 1987. Spanish military Model 47s were later designated Z-7A/Bs. The Brazilian Air Force used fifty-four H-13s, including four

This Westland-built Sioux AH Mk I was assigned to Great Britain's 3rd Royal Tank Regiment during 1969. (MAP)

This Model 47G was assigned to the Royal Hellenic (Greek) Air Force Training Wing during 1970. (MAP)

This was the first KH-4 (Bell 47G-3B) built under license by Kawasaki in Japan. The aircraft was on display at Johnson AFB, Japan during 1967. (Nick Williams)

This Westland-built Sioux of the Royal New Zealand Air Force was at Ohakea during May of 1987. (via Terry Love)

This Dark Gray and Olive Drab camouflaged Agusta Bell 47J was operated by the Italian Air Force. The aircraft was based at Bologna during 1978. (via Terry Love)

Model 47J Rangers, purchased in 1958 for the governorship, while the Navy operated ten Model 47s. The French Air Force, Army, Navy and Gendarmerie, flew a mix of more than 150 Model 47s, primarily 47Gs form 1951 to 1965. The Italian Air Force operated numerous Agusta 47G-2/Js, while the Army flew twelve Agusta 47G-3B-1s, seventeen 47Js, and a number of ex-U.S. Army OH-13Hs. The Italian Navy also used 47G/Js.

The Royal Australian Air Force used sixty-four Model 47Gs, some of which saw service in the Vietnam war. Early in the war, some of the H-13s acquired by the VNAF, besides those from the U.S., were believed to have come from the French government. The

Royal Thai Army was also the recipient of American H-13s which were supplemented by 47Gs obtained by the Thai government. H-13 variants also saw military service with the Royal Norweigan Air Force, Nationalist Chinese Air Force, the Army of Taiwan, and the Royal Danish Air Force. Nearly thirty found their way into the inventory of the Columbian Air Force and ten H-13s were added to the Venezuelan National Guard. The Turkish Army used a mix of fifty OH-13H and TH-13Ts. The Greek Air Force and Army employ nineteen H-13s and the Pakistan Army also maintains an aviation wing comprising H-13 types.

The Israeli Helicopter Squadron had thirteen

One major foreign operator of Model 47 variants was the Spanish military who designated their H-13s Z-7A/Bs. This H13G derivative flew into the 1980s. (via Terry Love)

42

This Spanish H-13 hybrid features an enlarged cockpit bubble, enlarged fuel tanks, and arched skid cross tubes. The fuselage and fuel tanks were painted Red while the remainder of the aircraft, including the skids and cockpit interior, was Medium Blue. The top of the bubble was painted Orange. (via Terry Love)

This Westland-built Sioux AH Mk 1 was assigned to the British "Blue Eagles." (MAP)

Agusta 47G-2s on hand during the 1960s. The Swedish Navy's first helicopter was a Model 47 leased from a commercial firm in September of 1951. West Germany's pilot training school received its first 47G-2 during 1957. The Luftwaffe operated a total of

A British Army Westland Sioux AT Mk I trainer. During the 1960s these aircraft were painted Olive Drab with Dayglo Orange panels on the fuel tank and bubble door. (Candid Aero-Files)

This Westland-built Sioux was flown by the Royal Air Force at RAF Biggin Hill during 1967. The aircraft carried an American Indian head painted on the fuel tanks. (Norm Taylor)

forty-five Model 47G-2s, fourteen of which were built by Bell and thirty-one by Agusta, which were withdrawn from service in the Spring of 1974. Other air arms that operated substantial numbers of H-13s include the Royal New Zealand Air Force (thirteen), Argentina (twenty), Mexico (twenty-four), Peru (thirty-five), and Paraguay (twenty).

Military versions of the Model 47 also served the governments of Jamaica, Iran, Burma, Libya, Chile, Iraq, Austria, Indonesia, Finland, Belgium, Kenya, Sri Lanka, Uganda, Dahomay, Madagascar, Tanzania, India, Zaire, Zambia, Zimbabwe, Ecuador, Morocco, Malta, Malaysia, Cuba, Iceland, South Korea, Netherlands, Philippines, Honduras, South Yemen, Uruguay , Senegal, Guatemala, and the Dominican Republic.

An OH-13G of the Luftwaffe's Pilot Training School during the Summer of 1981. The aircraft had a Yellow ventral fin and the trim around the bubble door was also Yellow. The fuel tanks and fuselage area behind the bubble doors were Orange, while the remainder of the aircraft was Black. (via Terry Love)

Special Projects

Sioux Scout: The dynamic success of Bell's AH-1G Hueycobra helicopter gunship had its roots in the H-13. The Sioux Scout was Bell Helicopter's concept demonstrator that bridged the gap between the early armed helicopter and the fully integrated gunship. During the late 1950s and early 1960s, Bell conducted numerous configuration studies to find the optimum armed helicopter design. These studies culminated with focus on a vertically-tiered, tandem-seating arrangement (for pilot and gunner) which offered excellent visibility, superior weapons coverage and minimal drag.

On 27 December 1962, Bell decided to build a flying mockup using proven H-13 components. Following completion during July of 1963, the aircraft underwent intense flight and weapons tests. In November, the Scout began a three year U.S. tour that laid the foundation for the Hueycobra, the world's first integrated weapons helicopter.

Designated the Model 207, the Sioux Scout was derived from a combination of OH-13S and Model 47J-2 components. The thirty-seven foot main rotor came from the OH-13S while a modified tail rotor, transmission, center section, and tail boom were from the 47J-2. Power was supplied by a supercharged Lycoming TVO 435-BIA piston engine that delivered 220 horsepower. The basic weight was 2,283 pounds, with a maximum weight of 3,000 pounds. The Model 207 could cruise at 95 mph and had a maximum speed of 125 mph. A pair of stub wings served as the mounting location for external stores and also served as "wet wings" capable of holding forty-three gallons of fuel, giving the Scout a range in excess of 200 miles. The aircraft was forty-three feet, seven inches long (including main rotor) and ten feet high.

The Scout pioneered the use of side arm controls for the gunner, while the pilot had

This was the predecessor to the famed line of Hueycobra gunships. The Model 207 Sioux Scout featured stub wings and a new nose section with tandem-seating and a twin M60 machine gun turret. Even with these modifications, the aircraft was still recognizable as a H-13 variant. (Bell)

The tandem tiered seating arrangement tested and developed on the Sioux Scout was carried over to the AH-1G Hueycobra, and became the standard seating arrangement for a whole generation of attack helicopters, both U.S. and foreign. (Bell)

standard flight controls. Dual hydraulics were installed and the unique fuselage combined box beams and honeycomb panels to form a rigid structure which minimized vibration and absorbed turret recoil. Muscle for the Sioux Scout consisted of an Emerson Electric turret housing a pair of 7.62MM machine guns. Rockets were also carried, but never fired from the Scout.

The Model 207 was found to be superior to the OH-13S in nearly every performance aspect except sufficient power, a glaring

Wearing the NASA emblem on the fuel tanks, this H-I3G was loaned to NASA from the Army to test the three-bladed rigid rotor concept during the early 1960s. (NASA)

The three-blade rigid rotor mast and hub assembly was installed on a modified ex-Army H-13G for testing by NASA. The flexible engine air intake is visible between the fuel tanks. Although assigned to NASA, the aircraft still carried military star and bar national insignias on the ventral fin and fuel tanks. (NASA)

drawback for an attack helicopter. Scores of evaluators who put the Scout through its paces recommended that the Army develop a turbine-powered Model 207 derivative. Bell complied with development of the Hueycobra which proved the concept of the Sioux Scout.

NASA H-13s: From 1960 to 1963, NASA conducted research of the hingeless rotor at its Langley Research Center, Langley, Virginia. NASA installed the Bell components, which incorporated a three-bladed rotor, on a H-13G supplied by the Army. The

The Vertol 76 tilt-wing Vertical Take-Off and Landing (VTOL) aircraft was built around a basic H-13 airframe. The original design used a standard H-13 cockpit bubble. The names of eleven test pilots are listed on the cockpit door in Black. (Boeing Vertol)

Developed during 1963, the "Wing Ding" investigated the possibilities of combining the agility of the helicopter with the load lifting capabilities of the airplane. Fifteen gallon fuel tanks were added to the wing tips and the rotor mast could be tilted for increased forward speed. (Smithsonian Institution)

This highly modified H-13G was used to make the first flight of a turbine-powered helicopter, under the designation XH-13F. The engine, a 280 shp Continental-Turbomeca ST-51-T-3 Artouste, was mounted adjacent to the rotor mast. (Bell)

aircraft emerged from an extensive test program showing favorable results over conventional articulated rotors.

Besides HTL-6s used to train astronauts, other NASA H-13s made contributions to the space program. During late 1967, Bell delivered three Lunar Landing Training Vehicles (LLTV) for the Apollo program. Powered by a massive turbofan engine plus twenty-four rockets, the two-ton machine incorporated a H-13 cockpit and canopy sections. Several astronauts flew the LLTVs throughout the late 1960s and one was destroyed in a crash in December of 1968. A total of fifteen H-13s were operated at NASA facilities for various projects from 1949 to 1973.

Vertol 76: Pioneered in 1957, this experimental aircraft was the first tilt-wing VTOL ever built. The Vertol 76 (VZ-2) was developed for the Army and Office of Naval Research and became the first tilt-wing to go through conversion from vertical flight to horizontal and back again. The first complete conversion flight was accomplished on 15

July 1958, followed by an extensive three-year flight test program, plus an advanced wing test period.

The Vertol 76 was built around a highly modified H-13 airframe with a complete cockpit. The cockpit bubble was later customized into a larger streamlined enclosure. The entire wing and both rotor-propellers could be tilted to a vertical position, enabling the hybrid to take off and land like a helicopter. The transition from hover to forward flight occurred as the wing and props were tilted forward to horizontal, allowing flight as a fixed-wing aircraft. Consequently, the 76 had unusual potential as a close support aircraft under terrain conditions that would rule out the use of less versatile aircraft.

The highly altered H-13 led to a number of state-of-the-art breakthroughs in tilt-wing technology. In 1965, the Vertol 76 was retired and placed among other aviation firsts at the Smithsonian Institution in Washington, D.C.

"Wing Ding:" Another aberration among the long line of Model 47s was this one-of-a-kind

49

experiment that had fixed wings attached to a Model 47G. The fixed wings were intended to bypass the helicopter's normal hover capability, enabling it to lift heavy payloads. Although the "Wing Ding" left the ground, the concept didn't and the aircraft was returned to its original configuration.

Turbine Power: In early 1955, Bell re-engined a military H-13G (52-7974) with a 280 shp Continental-Turbomeca XT-51-T-3 Artouste turbine. The experimental aircraft was designated XH-13F, and made the first flight of a turbine powered helicopter.

The designation HUL-1M (later UH-13R) identified a pair of HUL-1s experimentally fitted with Allison T63 turbine engines. One of those served as a test bed for an alternate engine to power the Army's budding Light Observation Helicopter (LOH) during late 1963. Bell installed a 250 shp Continental T65-T-1 turbine in the Navy helicopter as part of the Army funded program.

Rigid Rotor: In 1961, Bell Helicopter engineers developed rigid rotor technology to the point where it could be applied to a broad range of rotary-wing aircraft. The simple rigid rotor concept dates back to pioneer helicopter days when it was believed the system could replace articulated single-rotor arrangements. Not surprising, the H-13 had a part in the project. Bell conducted flight tests with rigid rotor-equipped Model 47s, beginning in 1957 and continued evaluating these platforms well into the 1960s.

NASA conducted research of the hingeless rotor from 1960 to 1963 at its Langley Research Center. Under an agreement with Bell, a rigid rotor system was delivered to the Langley site for installation on a H-13G supplied by the Army. Besides simplifying rotor components, the rigid rotor system resulted in markedly improved handling qualities and gave the aircraft an unlimited center of gravity. There was also a substantial reduction in rotor hub drag and high stress levels, plus maintenance was minimized.

This was one of two HUL-1Ms, which were standard HUL-1 airframes mated with a turbine engine. The pair was finished in overall Light Gull Gray and redesignated as UH-13Rs during 1962. BuNo 149838 was parked on the Bell Fort Worth (Arlington) facility during 1964. (Bell)